Table of Contents

Acknowledgements

This book is dedicated to my amazing student, whose name will remain anonymous, for understanding the power of his voice.
To make a long story short, while working in my classroom he approached me and asked "Why haven't you created something for males?" Our conversation penetrated my heart so, that I went to God in prayer about it. A few weeks later this activity workbook became the Edition Two of "The Life of a Butterfly" Personal Development Book Series Collection.

I would like to give a special thank you to Cordell Haynes and Jonathan Wolf, my fellow educators, for the time spent collaborating and giving me insight from a males perspective.

Introduction

Hello Eagle! If you are reading this that means you have decided to take the time to get to know yourself a little more. The activities in this book are engaging and fun. The activities will challenge you to take a look at yourself from within. Throughout the various activities in this book, you will be examining your heart, self- reflecting, addressing any negative thoughts and doing some self-discovering.

Below is a commitment statement. By signing your name below, you are making a promise to yourself that you will take out some time to learn every fascinating feather of your strong wings; symbolically meaning you're getting to know the details of yourself in which all encompasses the man you are now and becoming.

Now are you ready to get started?

I, _____ is making a **promise** and **commitment** to complete this activity workbook. I will start ____/_____/_____ and complete on the date, ___/____/____.

*****At the end of this book you will be awarded a certificate of completion.*****

The Significance of an Eagle

The eagle symbolizes great strength, leadership and vision. Its spreads its strong wings over the step into creation and fans the fire, encouraging growth of new matter. The eagle brings the message of renewed life. Life is nor black or white. Life is a combination of joys, laughs, tears, trajectories, testimonies, discoveries and various stages and journeys. It's okay to embrace and enjoy this process of developing into an even better you. We were born to withstand life's obstacles and soar as high as a eagle and even higher.

Self–Perception

- What are things that come to mind when I think about myself?

Words of Encouragement: *"You can't control how others may perceive you but you can control how you perceive yourself."* - Shellie Slack

Our **Self-Perception** determines our behavior. If we think we are inadequate, we act that way. If we think we are amazing, we will act that way. The pathway towards happiness and being your true self is determined by our own thinking, our own inner process, and our self-perception. According to Mountain State Centers for Independent Living, "Improving your self-image, like improving any skill, takes time and practice. Developing good self-esteem involves encouraging a positive (but realistic) attitude toward yourself and the world around you and appreciating your worth, while at the same time behaving responsibly towards others. Self-esteem isn't self-absorption; it's self-respect. By working from the inside out (focusing on changing your own way of thinking before changing the circumstances around you), you can build your self-esteem." The goal of this positive thinking is to give yourself a more positive self-concept, while seeing yourself honestly and accepting yourself, and removing the internal barriers that can keep you from doing your best.

<u>Objective:</u> The following activities in this section assist with identifying any negative thoughts and behaviors towards self and to promote a more positive perception of who you are.

Self-Portrait

(What are my thoughts about myself?)

1. Let's begin with how you view yourself. Take a long look in the mirror. In the face you will create below, I want you to write down the first three words that come to your thoughts when you take a look in the mirror. Were these words negative or positive? Now, list at least three features you like about your appearance and, at the most, three features you don't like. You can use words, draw pictures, or cut out magazine pictures.

Be honest with yourself. Rate your perception of how you view yourself, on a scale of 1-10; 10 being the greatest. _____. I gave myself a _____ because

_____

_____

_____

_____

_____

_____

_____

_____

_____

_____

_____

_____

_____

_____

_____

_____

_____

_____

_____

_____

_____

_____

_____

_____

Self-Perception
Activity: Two

Take the Test
(A Mountain State Centers for Independent Living assessment)

How positive is your self-image? Answer these true or false statements and find out your results.

1. My glass is always half-empty, not half-full. **T or F**
2. I'm always apologizing for things. **T or F**
3. I'm always telling myself I "should" be doing this or that. **T or F**
4. I constantly criticize myself. **T or F**
5. What other people think about me influences how I feel about myself. **T or F**
6. I am critical of my mistakes and relive them over and over. **T or F**
7. I always let the people who care about me down. **T or F**
8. I feel like I have the weight of the world on my shoulders. **T or F**
9. I feel as if a partial failure is as bad as a complete failure. **T or F**
10. I bend over backwards to please others. **T or F**
11. I am not sure I have done a good job unless someone else points it out. **T or F**
12. It's hard for me to forgive and forget. **T or F**
13. I have to work harder than others for relationships and am afraid that the relationships I have will fail. **T or F**
14. If I don't do as well as others, it means that I am not as good as them. **T or F**
15. If I can't do something well, there is no point in doing it at all. **T or F**

Results

Give yourself one point for each question you answered with a "true". Add them up and match with the scale below.

0 - 4: You have a generally positive way of thinking and should feel good about yourself. Keep it up! If you are borderline with a 4 you might want to monitor those areas.

5 - 8: You may be struggling with some negative emotions. Take time to review your good qualities. Write them down on an index card. Use what you wrote on your index card as a daily affirmation and recite daily.

9 or more: You can be very critical of yourself. Challenge yourself to change your way of thinking by first, completing this workbook and apply the tools given in your life!

"Who Am I "

Personally, I've found that there is no one else like me or you, anywhere. Know that there are no duplicates of your DNA. Out of the billions of people here on the earth, there is ONLY one YOU; so embrace your uniqueness. Fill out the following questionnaire as open and honest as possible on the lines provided below to discover more about your uniqueness.

1. In general, I feel school is

_____

2. My best friend is_____

3. The one thing I like best about my class

_____

4. Something I'd like to tell my teacher

_____

_____

5. I don't like it when people

_____

_____

6. I'm at my best when I

_____

_____

7. Right now I feel

_____

because_____

8. I trust people when

_____

_____

_____

9. The best thing that could happen to me is

_____

10. When I don't like something I've done, I

_____

_____

_____

_____

_____

11. When I like something I've done, I

_____

_____

_____

_____

_____

12. When I'm proud of myself, I

_____

_____

_____

_____

13. I'm very happy that

_____

_____

_____

_____

_____

14. I wish my parents knew

_____

_____

_____

_____

15. Someday I hope

_____

_____

_____

_____

16. I would like to take a trip to

_____

_____

_____

17. Five adjectives that describe physical attributes and my characteristics are

_____

_____

_____

_____

_____

18. Five adjectives that describe my personality

_____

_____

_____

_____

19. I am a good friend because

_____

_____

_____

_____

_____

20. When I am sad I

_____

_____

21. I feel irritated when

_____

because_____

_____

_____

_____

22. My favorite book to read is

_____

23. My favorite movie to watch is

_____

Self-Perception
Activity: Four

"When they look at me, what do they see?"

Sometimes, the way we may perceive ourselves may come from how other's may view us. We have the tendency to take on others negative perceptions of ourselves to be true. Also, learning how others perceive us can be a mirror for us. It can become a moment of self-reflection and the opportunity to become aware of actions and behaviors we may need to work on or this can become an opportunity to discover and learn some great things about ourselves that makes us unique! With this activity, you can either interview your friends or family members or you can go by what you may already know.

In the boxes below fill in the words, scenarios, statements that were said by others. Include the person's name and relationship with you (friend, cousin, teacher, etc.)

New attributes, talents or gifts I learned about myself from others.	Negative Opinions from others that I have made my truth.	Positive things others have said about me.	Things I became aware of by others that I will reflect on.

Self-Perception
Activity: Five

New Self-Portrait
(New and Improved Self-Portrait)

By the end of this section, you should have identified some negative thoughts that you may have about who you are. Those thoughts may have come from yourself or others. Write down all of those negative thoughts right now on a separate sheet of paper. Once you have the list of negative thoughts, ball it up and throw it away. This is symbolically stating that you release those harmful ideas and that you will no longer perceive yourself in that way. Now, recreate your picture from activity one on the template provided on the next page. This picture should reflect a new and improved perception of yourself.

Directions: Write a list of at least 5 features you like about your appearance as well as write 10 positive words/affirmations that describe you. Now decorate your portrait. Be sure to use color. Cut out and place on your wall! (Use this activity as a reminder of how amazing you truly are!!!!)

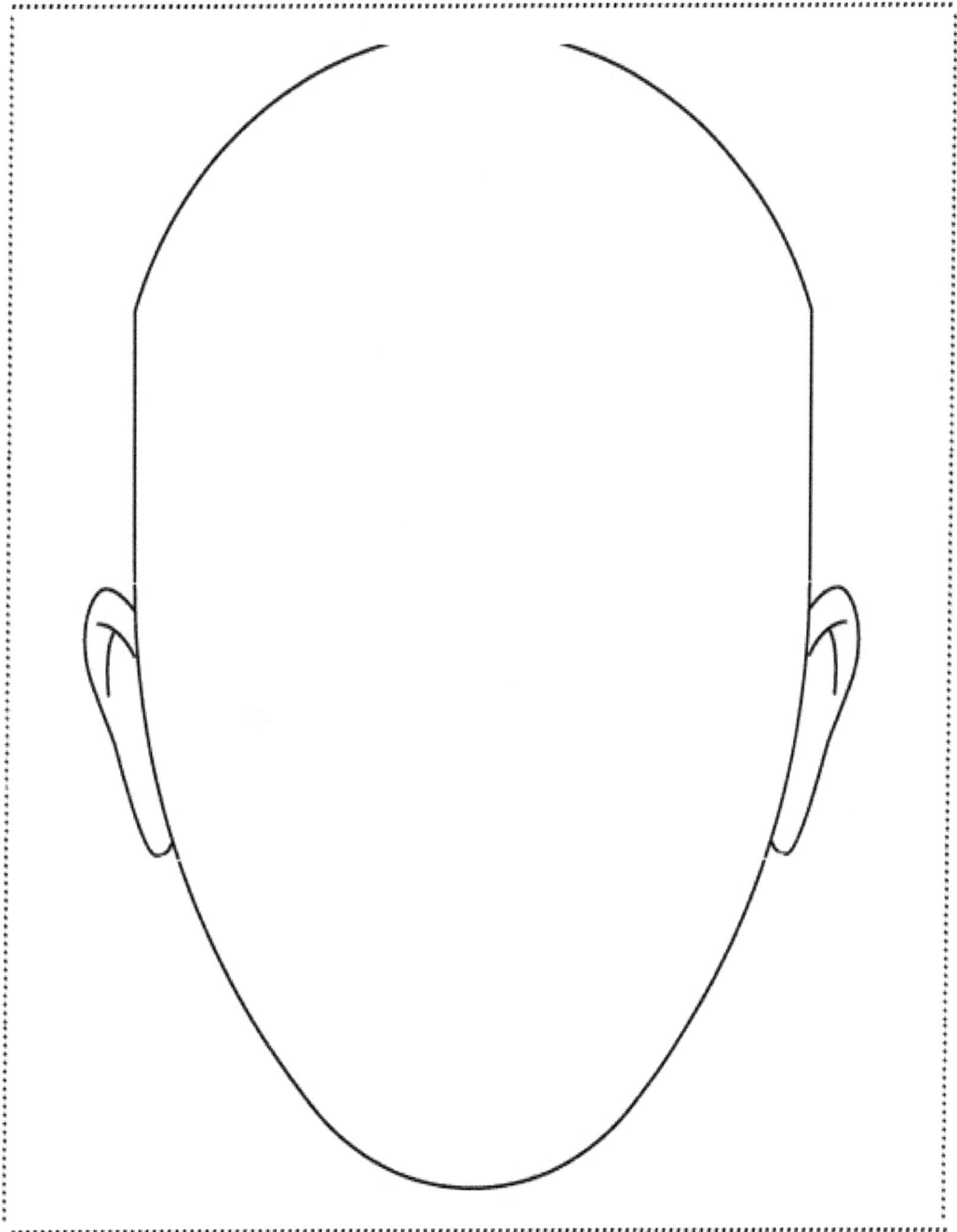

17

Self-Acceptance

FOCUS QUESTION – Have I accepted all of me? The good, the bad and the ugly?

Words of Encouragement - "We must accept everything about ourselves in order to begin to love ourselves fully; therefore, the way we show love to others will reflect the love we have for ourselves." – Unknown

"I acknowledge and accept everything about myself; the things I can change and the things that I can't." – Shellie Slack

"Self-Acceptance is the beginning process towards Self- Love." – Shellie Slack

> If self-acceptance is very difficult,
> see the needy child within.
> F or we all carry our children
> locked safely away.
> ~ © Alison Stormwolf ~

Objective: This section is designed for you to identify your strengths and weaknesses, as well as to start the process of accepting all of who you are.

Self-Acceptance

Do I acknowledge and accept everything about myself? The good/bad, imperfections and strengths/weaknesses.

1. Now take a deep look from within and list at least 8 things that you **LIKE** about yourself in each category below:

Characteristics *Ex: Nice*	Talents/Gifts *Ex: Dancing*	Strengths *Ex: Work well w/ others*

2. Part of Self-Acceptance includes accepting the things in our lives and about ourselves that are beyond our control. For example; the family we might be born into or facial features we are born with are both things that are beyond our control. It's important to realize that the things that are beyond our control have significance and purpose! Self-reflect and identify the things that you **DON'T** like but **CAN'T** change (Remember, these are the things beyond your control) and also reflect on what you **DON'T** like but with time **CAN** change, (EX. your circumstances, a mis-communication, areas of weakness or bad habits). Now, write them down on the lines provided below.

Don't Like and Can't Change	Don't Like and Can Change

Proud Moments

It's important to acknowledge the moments in life that you may be proud of. Take a moment to enjoy expressing pride in something you have done that might have gone unrecognized. It is sometimes difficult for people to actually say, *"I'm proud that I…."* Make a statement about a specific topic below, beginning with "I'm proud that I….". Below are some suggested topics for use in this exercise:

1.Things you've done for your parent(s) or guardian: **I am proud that I** …

_____

_____

_____

_____

_____

_____

2.Things you've done for a friend: **I am proud that I**………..

_____

_____

_____

_____

_____

_____

3. Work in school: **I am proud that I** ………..

_____

_____

_____

_____

_____

_____

4. How you spend your time outside of school: **I am proud that I** …………

_____

_____

_____

_____

_____

_____

5. About your religious beliefs: **I am proud that I**………………

_____

_____

_____

_____

_____

_____

6. How you've earned some money: **I am proud that I**…………

_____

_____

_____

_____

_____

7. Something you've bought recently: **I am proud that I** ………….

_____

_____

_____

_____

_____

_____

_____

8. Good habits you have: **I am proud that I**..............

_____

_____

_____

_____

_____

9. Something you do often: **I am proud that I**...........

_____

_____

_____

_____

10. What you are proudest of in your life: **I am proud that**.........

_____

_____

_____

11. Something you have shared: **I am proud that I**...............

_____

_____

_____

_____

12. Something you tried hard for: **I am proud that I**............

_____

_____

_____

_____

13. A class you earned a good grade in: **I am proud that I** ....

_____

_____

_____

_____

14. Thoughts about people who are different from you: **I am proud that I** ...

_____

_____

_____

_____

15. Something you've done to help someone else: **I am proud that I**

_____

_____

_____

_____

_____

_____

Change

DIRECTIONS: Refer back to activity one, number two. You were asked to write down some things that you **did not** like but with time, you wanted to start making **some necessary changes.** In the box below write your goals and a brief description of your plan of execution.

Suggestions:

- Your habits
- Your grades
- Your attitude

Changes I Want To Make	Steps I Can Take To Make The Changes
Ex. I want to begin to turn in my ALL of my homework.	Ex. Instead of watching T.V. as soon as I get home, my homework will be the first thing to complete before I watch T.V or play video games.

Pot of Gold

Now it is time to reflect. What are you beginning to discover about yourself? What are some things you need to accept about the person you are now? Give yourself a pat on the back at this very moment. You are doing great with accepting all of who you are with the desire to work on you and develop even more.

Directions: In the big pot of gold coins on the next page, Write down all the things you accept about yourself inside the pot of gold and all of the things you will work on towards accepting about yourself outside of the pot. Use this activity as a reminder that this is a journey and it is a process towards progress.

Self-Acceptance
Activity: Five

Say it Out Loud

Refer to activity one again. Look at the things you **DON'T** like that you **CAN'T**
change (Beyond your control) and where you see that it best fits, write them in the blanks
below: Recite this affirmation daily, until you begin to believe it!

*"TODAY I declare, that I will begin to Accept ALL of me! I
will work on the things I can change and accept the things that I
can't. I don't like_____ but I accept
it, acknowledging and believing that I am created perfect the way I
am. I don't like_____
but I accept it, with the belief that it has purpose. I don't
like_____ but I accept it. I believe
that I am on the path to greatness! I do not strive for perfection
but I strive to be the BEST that I can be. I am perfectly imperfect.
There is no one on earth exactly like ME and that makes me
special and unique."*

Self-Devotion

FOCUS QUESTION - How much am I spending time to develop myself? Do I show myself love?

Words of Encouragement: "Self-Love is a continual process. One minute you can be committed to being a better person by showing love towards yourself like no other and then you may encounter an off day, a bad week or month due to other factors. The key is to become self-aware, do a self-check in (a look from within), and evaluate those times when you are not loving yourself to the fullest. Each of our journeys towards self-devotion is individually unique."   -Shellie Slack

"You yourself, as much as anybody in the entire universe, deserve your love and affection" - Unknown

"A person cannot be comfortable in his own skin without his own approval."

- Unknown

Objective: The self-devotion activities are created for you to identify exactly where you are currently along your journey towards self-love and to learn and discover various ways to show your love.

Self-Devotion
Activity: One

Rate Yourself

(How do I feel about myself?)

1. Rate how much you love yourself on a scale of 1-10; 10 being the greatest. _____. How do you measure self-love for yourself? It's different for everyone. Loving yourself is a daily intention that can change day by day. It is important that we do routine self checks of loving ourselves.

2. Take a moment to think about a time or at times when you feel the most loved. In the box below; draw an illustration of that moment and describe your picture on the lines provided on the next page.

Real Men Show Self-Love

I love myself

because_____

The self-love tree is an activity that promotes self-love through self-expression.

Directions: From the roots of the tree to its leaves, label the tree, using words, draw symbols or pictures that express how much you love yourself.

May the love for yourself, continue to grow!

Self-Devotion
Activity: Three

Charts of Hearts

Directions: Fill in the blanks. Draw a star inside of the boxes that resonates with you the most.

I show myself love when I....	I show love to others when	The last time I showed myself love I did....	When I think of love, the color I see is....
I think its thoughtful when others...	My favorite pair of shoes to wear....	My favorite Birthday memory was when....	My Dream trip is to...
The type of books I like to read is. ...	My favorite music artist is....	My favorite sports team is....	My favorite outfit in my closet is....

I embrace ___ about myself…	I will forgive ___for	I will stop worrying about. …	I need to heal from...

Self-Devotion
Activity: Four

Be Still

(This is a meditation activity where you will be visualizing your best self NOW and the person you are 10 years from now)

Step 1: Read through these directions twice before you start so that you do not have to interrupt your meditation session.

Step 2: Find a nice quiet space in your house, your room or outdoors and lay down on your back. You have the choice to listen to nature sounds in the background or just lay in silence.

Step 3: Close your eyes and begin to focus your thoughts on your breath. Listen to yourself breathe. Pay attention to the rhythm of your breathing patterns. Are you breathing fast or slow? If you are breathing fast, try slowing down by taking a longer deep breath in and out twice.

Step 4: Begin to envision yourself now. What does your best self look like? What are you doing? How are you encouraging others? What are some nice words that come to thought about who you are as your best self? What are you wearing? Are you smiling? Do you look a lot happier? What surrounds you that brings you joy?

Step 5: Now envision the person you have become 10 years from now. Is it an extension of the best version of yourself you'd envisioned? What career or business do you have? What type of volunteer work are you doing in the community? What are you passionate about? Where do you live? What kind of car do you drive? Do you have any kids?

Directions: On the next page, write down /illustrate what you envisioned during meditation in the box.

My Best Self Now	The Person I will be in 10 Years

Daily Self-Love Check-in

Date:

Today I feel like…and why?

_____

_____

_____

_____

No matter how I may feel today, I love myself today because…

_____

_____

_____

_____

Something nice I said to myself today was..

_____

_____

_____

Something nice I did for myself today was...

_____

_____

_____

_____

Self-Devotion

Daily Self-Love Check-in

Date:

Today I feel like...and why?

_____

_____

_____

_____

No matter how I may feel today, I love myself today because...

_____

_____

_____

_____

Something nice I said to myself today was..

_____

_____

_____

_____

Something good I did for myself today was...

_____

_____

_____

_____

Self-Devotion

Daily Self-Love Check-in

Date:

Today I feel like…and why?

_____

_____

_____

_____

No matter how I may feel today, I love myself today because…

_____

_____

_____

_____

Something nice I said to myself today was..

_____

_____

_____

_____

Something good I did for myself today was...

_____

_____

_____

_____

Self-Devotion

Daily Self-Love Check-in

Date:

Today I feel like…and why?

_____

_____

_____

_____

No matter how I may feel today, I love myself today because…

_____

_____

_____

_____

Something nice I said to myself today was..

_____

_____

_____

_____

Something good I did for myself today was...

_____

_____

_____

_____

Self-Devotion

Daily Self-Love Check-in

Date:

Today I feel like…and why?

_____

_____

_____

_____

No matter how I may feel today, I love myself today because…

_____

_____

_____

_____

Something nice I said to myself today was..

_____

_____

_____

_____

Something good I did for myself today was...

_____

_____

_____

_____

_____

Self-Devotion

Daily Self-Love Check-in

Date:

Today I feel like...and why?

_____

_____

_____

_____

No matter how I may feel today, I love myself today because...

_____

_____

_____

_____

Something nice I said to myself today was..

_____

_____

_____

_____

Something good I did for myself today was...

_____

_____

_____

_____

Self-Devotion

Daily Self-Love Check-in

Date:

Today I feel like…and why?

_____

_____

_____

_____

No matter how I may feel today, I love myself today because…

_____

_____

_____

_____

Something nice I said to myself today was..

_____

_____

_____

_____

Something good I did for myself today was...

_____

_____

_____

_____

Self-Devotion

Daily Self-Love Check-in

Date:

Today I feel like…and why?

_____

_____

_____

_____

No matter how I may feel today, I love myself today because…

_____

_____

_____

_____

Something nice I said to myself today was..

_____

_____

_____

_____

Something good I did for myself today was...

_____

_____

_____

_____

Self-Devotion

Daily Self-Love Check-in

Date:

Today I feel like…and why?

_____

_____

_____

_____

No matter how I may feel today, I love myself today because…

_____

_____

_____

_____

Something nice I said to myself today was..

_____

_____

_____

_____

Something good I did for myself today was...

_____

_____

_____

_____

Self-Devotion

Daily Self-Love Check-in

Date:

Today I feel like…and why?

_____

_____

_____

_____

No matter how I may feel today, I love myself today because…

_____

_____

_____

_____

Something nice I said to myself today was..

_____

_____

_____

_____

Something good I did for myself today was...

_____

_____

_____

_____

Self-Devotion

BONUS

<u>FOCUS QUESTION</u>: Because I am choosing to love myself, how do I imagine my love towards others?

1. In your opinion, what does a true friendship look like to you?

_____

_____

_____

_____

_____

2. Are you reflecting the type of son, cousin, uncle, person, and friend you would like to be surrounded by? Are you the type of person you would want in your own life? Why or why not?

_____

_____

_____

_____

_____

3. What are some ways you can show your family and friends you love them.

_____

_____

_____

_____

4. Refer to additional activities, **"15 Great Self Esteem Building Exercise for Teens"** Written by Zdravko Lukovski :

http://enlightenmentportal.com/development/self-esteem-building-activities/

Self-Discovery

FOCUS QUESTION: Who am I and what am I put on this earth to do?

Words of encouragement: "You were born to do AMAZING things here on the earth. You have so many gifts and talents that you have yet discovered. Your gifts and talents are comparable to small golden nuggets, that are hidden treasures ready to be discovered and utilized by you. Your gifts and talents help add color to the world." –Shellie Slack

" LIFE IS AN ENDLESS PROCESS OF SELF-DISCOVERIES."- James Gardner

"There are two great days in a person's life. The day they are born and the day they discover why?" - William Barclay

"The Greatest Discovery of all is that a man can CHANGE his FUTURE by merely changing his MIND and his ATTITUDE." - Unknown

Objective: The activities in this self-discovery section will create a space for reflection and finding your purpose.

The Masks

Do you often compare yourself to others? Many people compare themselves to others and they also wear different masks. According to Child Psychologist, Dr. Kate L. Truitt, wearing a mask allows people to change how they act; depending on the norms of the social situation they are in. The masks may provide a comforting way for them to hide their true selves and fit in as well as they may serve as a protective barrier to avoid getting hurt. People tend to feel that it is easier to hide behind the mask instead of being confident and comfortable enough to be themselves. As teenagers, you probably go through experiences of an unbalance of emotions at times, that may leave you feeling more vulnerable to loss of identity. This activity allows you to self-reflect, analyze and explore the different in which ways you might act around people in your life.

Materials:

-   Paper plates (Total of 3)

-   Magazines or Construction paper

-   Pencils or pens, colored markers

-   Scissors, glue or tape

Instructions:

How do you act at school, home and social events and around your parents or guardians, friends, boys, girls, strangers, teachers, sports coaches and others? Think about the masks you may wear and how they might change daily.

_____

_____

_____

_____

_____

_____

Be creative and decorate three masks. Each mask should represent the top 3 ways you present yourself the most to others.

On the lines provided below write about your masks and how they change from day to day and situation to situation. Which mask do you feel the most comfortable in? Which mask would you take off for good? Which masks is mostly who you truly are? What have you discovered about yourself? How would you take what you learned about yourself in this activity and apply it to your daily life?

_____

_____

_____

_____

_____

_____

_____

_____

_____

_____

_____

Self-Discovery
Activity: Two

Purpose

The graphic organizer provided below will help you have clarity of your purpose as well as provide a visual of the connection between who you are, what you like to do, the activities you may be involved in and your passions. This graphic organizer can also be a Self-Check-In on how much time you spend on activities that are not contributing to the person you want become.

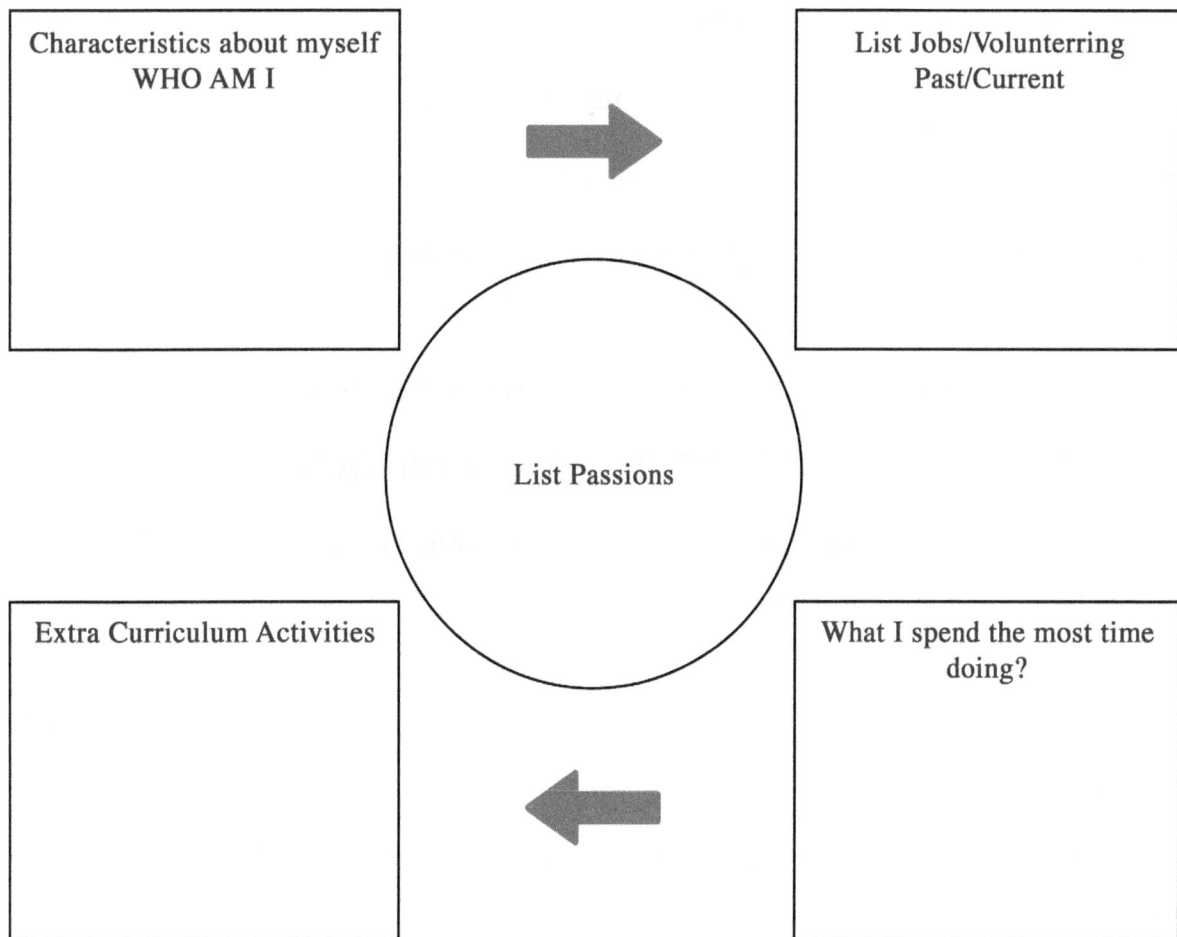

Characteristics about myself WHO AM I	List Jobs/Volunterring Past/Current

List Passions

Extra Curriculum Activities	What I spend the most time doing?

Personal Mission Statement

A personal mission statement is a statement that explains what you stand for in the world as well as explains who you are and who you want to become. Your personal statement can be used to help guide you when making choices and decisions in life as well as hold you accountable for who you stated you are and what you want to become by asking yourself, "Does this choice help me become the person I want to be?"

Self-Reflect: What imprint would you like to make in the world? Your personal mission statement should answer 4 questions:

1) What is my life currently about—what is my life's purpose?

2) What do I stand for - what are my core values?

3) What accomplishments am I working towards that will help me fulfill my life's purpose in a manner consistent with my core values?

4) Will my daily habits help me progress towards the future I desire?

STEP 1: *IDENTIFY YOUR PURPOSE AND CORE VALUES*

A. As you may have discovered in previous activities; write a list of at least 3 talents you have and describe how your talents are able to help others.

_____

_____

_____

B. Self-Reflect: What excites you about your life? About the world? What angers you about your life? About the world?

_____

_____

_____

_____

_____

_____

_____

_____

_____

_____

_____

_____

C. What would you like to change about the world? How would you help change things? What would you be doing? In detail; Can you describe the cause? Imagine it—and just write it down even though you might feel the vision is too big for you. Just Dream Big!

_____

_____

_____

_____

_____

_____

_____

_____

_____

_____

_____

_____

_____

_____

D. Imagine that you just turned **30+** years old, and you are at an red carpet awards event about to be honored by Barack Obama. Imagine yourself at the podium holding the mike. What will your acceptance speech say? On the lines below, include what you have done. What would your friends, the people you work with, family members say about you? What difference would you hope you had made in their lives; in the world? How do you want to be remembered?

_____

_____

_____

_____

_____

_____

_____

_____

_____

_____

E. It is important to instill wisdom into the generation before you; the youth. Now, imagine yourself to be standing in front of middle school students in a classroom, giving some words of wisdom? What advice would you give them about school? Going to High School? Their choice of friends? What would you tell them is important in life? Looking back on your life, what lessons you had learned would you share?

_____

_____

_____

_____

_____

_____

_____

STEP 2: *DRAFT YOUR PERSONAL MISSION STATEMENT*

Look over what you've written during Step 1. Then review the third question again (Letter C).

Write a rough draft of your personal mission statement in 40 words or less.

EX: Author's *Personal Mission Statement* – "I am on a Million Book Mission to help spread healing and inspiration around the world through my proclaimed self–help book, "The Life of A Butterfly; Secrets to Embracing Your Journey Into Womanhood ."

Now, Take the time to write your Personal Mission Statement below:

_____

_____

_____

_____

_____

_____

_____

_____

_____

_____

_____

You can keep your draft personal mission statement with you — see how it makes you feel. You may want to share it with someone who is a mentor or positive role model in your life. Revisit it at least once a month as a reminder and inspiration. As time passes, you may add to it or change it. Remember, you are creating the life you want to live.

Build an Eagle

Directions: Take the time to reflect. Get a piece of white paper. Draw a Eagle that is big enough to cover almost the entire paper. Draw lines on the wings making sections big enough to write in. Get a highlighter, colored pencils or crayons. In each section of your wings, write the following words;

- Kindness   Healing
- Patience   Confidence
- Selflessness   Discipline
- Worthiness   Empathy
- Self-Esteem   Habits
- Joy   Positive
- Peace   Ambitious
- Self-Love   Assertiveness
- Self- Awareness   Self-Control
- Purpose   Leadership
- Forgiveness   Happiness

Color the areas (words) on the Eagle in which you have obtained insight and/or growth. The sections of your wing you did not color will be areas to tackle along your journey and growth.

Morning AFFIRMATION

Look in the mirror and recite this morning affirmation daily! Be intentional when you start your day with positive thoughts that build your faith, creativity, and self-esteem! Make it a great one!

"I believe that I am great! I am powerful! I am loved. I am bold and confident. I have joy and peace; I am surrounded by love and positivity! I will give the world what I want in return, I will receive all that I need and more! I represent greatness, loyalty, and I respect others. I will be mindful of my thoughts and words towards others and myself. I will always do my best! I can achieve academic success and do whatever I put my mind to do, therefore I can become whoever I want to be!"

Certification of Completion!

Congratulations!!!! You have honored yourself by staying committed to completing this workbook. Use some of the tools provided in the book as a reference and reminder of the man that you are striving to become. Remember to embrace every one of your imperfections because you are perfectly imperfect. You were BORN to Fly, So, **Soar High like an Eagle!** The next page presents your certificate of completion. Cut out your certificate and be sure to frame it. **YOU DID IT!!!!**

CERTIFICATE *of* COMPLETION

THIS ACKNOWLEDGES

_____

_____

FOR YOUR COMMITMENT TOWARDS BECOMING A MASTER OF YOUR OWN SELF- PERCEPTION!
"SOAR HIGH EAGLE!"

The Life of a Butterfly

Shellie Slack

SIGNED, *Shellie Slack. Author*

Resource Page

1. Self- Perception **Activity #2 Self-Perception-Take the Test** (A Mountain State Centers for Independent Living assessment)

2. *Self-Love* ***BONUS Activity #4 Written by Zdravko Lukovski***
   http://enlightenmentportal.com/development/self-esteem-building-activities/

3. If you are battling with Suicide; Call Hotline **800-273-8255**

"The International Association for Suicide Prevention works with the World Health Organization every year to host the World Suicide Prevention Day on September 10. Over 800,000 people commit suicide across the world each year, notes the IASP. As such, it encourages people to take a day to raise awareness about suicide, the factors that drive people to commit suicide and the methods of prevention."

4. ***Need Someone To Talk to?*** Online therapy and counseling for Anxiety, Depression, Drug/Alcohol Use, Grief and Loss Relationships and Trauma.

Call Telehealth –(866) 740-6502; USC Suzanne Dworak-Peck –School of Social Work